7 Tips for Buying a Used Car

Background

First car sales job

My first job in the car business was back in 1986. I was working at a radio station on the overnight shift and it didn't pay enough to live on. I went to a dealership that was advertising an opening for a salesman and they were more than happy to give me a shot. There was almost no training and on the second day I started taking Ups. I'm not sure about the origin of that jargon, it probably comes from sales managers yelling at salesmen "get up off your butt, there's a customer at the door."

This may sound silly, but it is not unusual. There is a very good chance that the salesperson you meet at the dealership has very little if any experience. Typical turnover among car salespeople is very high at most dealerships because there is a sink or swim culture. Dealerships are required to pay a minimum hourly rate, but if your commissions don't exceed your pay within a couple of months, you will be fired. When you arrive at the dealership, your salesperson will either be the seasoned vet who knows how to "hold gross" in the deal, the guy or gal on the bubble who has to make another sale to keep their job, or the greenhorn who has yet to prove themselves.

Which one do you want? You will get the best deal from the salesperson on the bubble. The seasoned vet is confident of their numbers and they want to maintain the higher profit margin that swells their paycheck. The greenhorn is simply a conduit to the sales manager and doesn't have the pull to sell your offer to the boss. The only thing sales managers hate worse than getting chewed out for not making their sales targets is breaking in a new greenhorn, so approving a deal with a thin margin to help a salesperson on the bubble means another month without that headache.

Figuring out who is which is really easy. The vet has plaques on the wall, gold stars on their business card, pictures of their kids on the desk, and enough swagger for three. The greenhorn is still a little confused and has to ask other salespeople questions about how to use their accounting software and is overly eager to take you on the test drive. The ones on the bubble are everyone else.

I never made it to the bubble at that first dealership. I got lost on a test drive with a customer at the end of my first week and was so embarrassed that I quit.

CarMax

My second job in the car business was thirteen years later after college and grad school. Circuit City had started a division that was trying to apply the big box retail model to used car sales and they needed a market research manager. When they hired me there were five locations and they were still trying to figure things out. Initially, my role was simply to conduct customer satisfaction surveys with the people who bought a car from CarMax, but that quickly expanded to many other areas. Measuring customer reaction was the common thread to all of this research work. We tested reaction to the advertising, showroom design, service operations, new store locations, and sales process. During nearly a decade with CarMax, I gathered information either personally, through surveys, or through sales data from over two million retail and service customers.

Carfax

In 2007, I left CarMax and joined Carfax. While CarMax had become one of the biggest used car retailers in the world, Carfax is actually involved in millions more used car transactions. CarMax serves a very specific type of customer while Carfax serves customers across the entire spectrum of used car sales. My job was to understand all those different types of customers and the different types of sellers they were dealing with. While CarMax tries to make every used car they sell meet a certain standard, most used cars have very unique characteristics based on how and where they have been driven and how diligent their prior owners have been keeping them maintained.

In the last few years, I've learned a lot about how car buyers react to these unique vehicle histories and how those reactions impact the perceived value of each individual used car. While you may not care whether the car you are buying started its life as a rental car and has had owners in three different states along the Gulf coast, the people you will eventually sell the car to will very likely demand a discount. On the other hand, if the car had only one prior owner who changed the oil every three thousand miles, you can expect to get a premium price when you sell it.

Twenty years of working in the car business, looking at millions of transactions across thousands of dealerships and private party sales gives me a unique perspective that I am eager to share with you. In fact, after reading this book, you will have a better understanding of the nature of this business than many of the car salespeople you will encounter.

Table Stakes

Most of the guidebooks and articles about buying a used car spend a lot of time talking about the basics. I'm not going to waste your time going into great detail about these common sense practices. Everyone buying a used car should go through these steps, but there is nothing novel or creative about these recommendations so I don't include them in my seven tips.

Needs

Think about how you are going to use the vehicle. If you are driving alone on a long daily commute, don't look at gas guzzling pickup trucks or SUVs. If you frequently go camping places with unpaved roads, get a four wheel drive vehicle with good ground clearance. Taking half the soccer team to the pizza joint to celebrate a victory? You need a third row seat in a minivan or SUV. Obvious, right?

Budget

Your vehicle should enhance your quality of life, not detract from it. Stressing over the monthly car payment or giving up restaurants and movies to drive a fancy car is silly. Your car payment should be a maximum of twenty percent of your take home pay.

Cars are machines and machines break. If you have too much of your budget devoted to making the payment, you may not be able to afford the repairs when the vehicle inevitably breaks down. Instead of buying a car with a $450 monthly payment, get one with a $350 monthly payment and put the extra $100 in a savings account for fifteen months. Then when the car has a $1,500 repair bill, you'll have the money to cover it and will be back on the road.

Pricing Research

Decades ago, you would have to comb through the newspaper classified ads to try and figure out a fair price for the vehicle you were considering. You could try and get your hands on a printed version of the guide books insurance companies and taxing authorities used to value vehicles, but they were vague and often outdated. Then came the internet, but the early listing sites were simply electronic versions of the printed ads.

Today, information about available vehicles and their value is everywhere. Most of the listing sites provide links to electronic pricing guides or have their own analytic models to compare the vehicle asking price to an estimated value. This service has taken the guesswork out of the process for anyone who takes the time to do their homework.

The weakness for nearly all of the valuation tools is their level of analysis. You can find a value estimate based on the make, model, model year, mileage, and region from at least four reputable sources. This means you will get the same value estimate for all of the 2012 Toyota Corollas with fifty thousand miles in Dallas. There is only one pricing model that estimates the value of a vehicle at the level of the individual vehicle accounting for that vehicle's unique vehicle history. Carfax can tell you the market value of the 2012 Toyota Corolla with fifty thousand miles, three owners, an accident, and no oil changes. Until Carfax decides to license their vehicle history data to other pricing services, they are the only source for this vehicle specific price reference.

Tip 1 - Understand the deal

Four square

There are four ways a car dealer makes money on a used car sale

- The difference between the price and how much the dealer has in the car
- The difference between the trade-in and what he can sell the trade for
- The financing revenue
- The profit on "extras"

Most used car buyers only think about the first box in the four square. If the dealer bought the car for $10,000 and spent $1,000 getting it ready to sell, then they have $11,000 in the car. If you could buy that car for $11,200, you might think you got a great deal.

However, if you are also trading in a car, the dealer knows what he can get for the car at auction and will try to increase profits by getting you to accept a much lower value for your trade. The wholesale values offered by pricing guides give you a rough idea of what the dealer can expect to get for your trade, but there will be transportation costs and auction fees eating into his profit. A dealer will usually "step up" on a vehicle he can expect to recondition and retail on his own lot.

Your choice if you have a trade-in is whether to sell it yourself at a price closer to retail, or avoid the hassle of dealing with buyers and paperwork and accept a wholesale value. Just be aware that the dealer's offer for your trade will be low enough to cover all the costs of reconditioning and marketing.

The third and least obvious way the dealer makes money on the used car sale is financing. Remember, when you are buying a used car with a finance contract, you are also buying money. That money has a price and the dealer will either collect the entire profit of the money contract by financing the purchase outright, or will collect a finder's fee from the lender who underwrites the deal. This profit is recorded in the paperwork but takes a keen eye and some foreknowledge to discover.

The dealer may also offer to lease you the car to get lower monthly payments. Used car leasing is typically reserved for late-model low mileage vehicles from long-lasting brands with high residual values. Do not use leasing as a way to get a more expensive car at a monthly payment you can afford. Leasing a car is not buying a car, it is simply paying to use a car for a fixed period of time. A leased car belongs to someone else and you have to follow their rules to use their car or pay a high penalty. That means you have limitations on how many miles you can drive, how often you get the vehicle serviced, and how you treat the interior. It also means that in a couple of years, you will have to turn in the car and be right back in the same situation, only this time you will not have a trade-in. If the doctor has given you one year to live and you want to drive a fancy car, go ahead and use a lease, otherwise buy the car you can actually afford.

If you cannot pay cash for the used car, your best option is to use a credit union to finance your purchase. Credit unions almost always have the cheapest money for car purchases and will often give you a further discount if you sign up for automatic payment through an existing account. Take advantage of this option if it is available to you. If you are in a situation where no other lender will sell you the money to buy a car, many dealers will carry the note. These dealers are generally referred to as buy-here pay-here dealers.

You will pay very high interest rates and may be required to make a large down payment at a buy-here pay-here dealership. You will be required to make your payments on a timely basis or face losing the vehicle. Normal car loans have a ten day grace period, buy-here pay-here dealers may give you a couple of days. These dealers expect a high percentage of their customers to default on their loans and will often install tracking devices on the vehicle to facilitate repossession.

Dealers also have arrangements with sub-prime lenders who will finance high risk customers, but at a high price. Your credit score will determine how much you have to pay for the money to buy the car, so do everything you can to drive up that score before you begin the purchase process. The difference between a 580 credit score and a 780 credit score can be thousands of dollars in finance costs.

If you are paying cash or have pre-arranged financing with a credit union, that is one less way the dealer can make money so they will press hard to make more profit in the fourth box of the four square: extras.

The most aggressive salesperson at a dealership is typically the F&I manager. This person is responsible for adding profit to the used car transaction by selling you things you don't need at a very high margin. They typically follow an assumptive sales process and simply add the extras to your contract before you have a chance to opt out. You have negotiated a purchase price on the vehicle and you have every right to say "no thank you" to extras like security etching, fabric protection, under coating, lifetime oil changes, extended service contracts, etc.

If you are relying on the dealership for financing, they may require a finance insurance policy akin to the mortgage insurance you get when you buy a house. This insurance is available outside of the dealership at much better rates, which is another great reason to have your financing arranged before you make your purchase.

The typical customer who arrives at the dealership unarmed with this information will typically generate over four thousand dollars in profit for the dealership on an average used car. Now that you know the four squares, you should be able to escape without paying more than a thousand over dealer cost.

Business model

Car dealers are selling a depreciating asset. Every day that a vehicle sits on their lot, it loses value. Austin Ligon, the original CEO of CarMax once told his store managers "you are selling bananas." His point was the vehicles have a limited shelf life, and if they are not sold in time, they will have to be disposed of. CarMax still follows this principle and will sell off aged inventory to other car dealers.

In many cases, dealers use someone else's money to finance their inventory so they are both losing the value of the vehicle and paying a finance charge. There is often a thirty-day float in these finance arrangements, called floor planning, so the dealer has a strong incentive to sell the car within the first month so they can transfer the balance to a new vehicle and restart the clock.

However, car dealers hate giving away money. If a car sells just days after they put it on their lot, they think they underpriced the vehicle. The typical practice is to initially list inventory at a higher price, assuming dozens of people have been waiting for a car just like this one to become available. This may have worked years ago, but so many cars are now listed online that this practice almost never works. Generally, they end up lowering the price after a couple of weeks to a point where they start to get inquiries.

Unlike CarMax, many dealers fail to realize that their most valuable asset is shelf space. A car taking up space on their lot is keeping another car from occupying that same space. If no one is asking about the car, or people are walking away from it after taking a test drive, that "dead" car is killing the dealer's bottom line. Often these cars are perfectly fine, but the dealer simply hasn't presented it well or kept it in pristine condition while it sat on his lot. If you find one of these vehicles, the dealer will be relieved to get rid of it and be willing to negotiate an attractive purchase price. You may even be able to negotiate a full cosmetic detail as part of the purchase. The Carfax report will typically tell you when the car was initially offered for sale by the dealer. Any vehicle that has been in a dealer's inventory more than three months is ripe for the picking.

Timing

Car dealers run their business with monthly goals. If they hit their numbers in week three, they are not going to offer big discounts in week four. Never buy a car in the first week of the month, though sometimes the first day of the month is considered the last day of the previous month and a dealer that needs one more sale to make his number may fudge the books.

The simplest way to take advantage of this phenomenon is to visit a dealership in week two or three and express mild interest in the car you want to buy, then leave, but give the salesman your contact info. Leaving a car dealership is not always simple. Be careful when you answer the inevitable question, "What can I do to sell you this car, today?" The correct answer to that question on your first visit is "Nothing, I'm looking at several cars at different dealerships and I'm not going to buy anything until I have seen them all." This does not make sense when shopping for new cars because they are all alike and the only difference is price, but for used cars it is completely logical.

You can also get held up at the dealership if you agree to an appraisal on your trade. Do not give someone else the keys to your car if you plan on leaving in less than four hours. Remember, your first visit is just to meet a salesman and test drive the car you might buy. After the test drive, say thanks and leave.

Then wait. If they call you before week four, that is a good sign, but tell them you are still looking and to check back in another week. If they call again in week four, then schedule a visit on the last day of the month. This gives you full leverage.

Tip 2 - Define winning

What are your expectations

Feeling good about a used car purchase requires that you set clear goals and achieve them. The first and most obvious goal should be getting the vehicle you actually want. This goal may evolve as you do your research and test drive some cars, but have the answer firmly in your head before you ever sign a contract. This is often more difficult than it seems. I bought a Dodge Caravan once because the Honda Odyssey I really wanted was gone, purchased by someone else that morning. Instead of just leaving, we test drove a couple of other vehicles and settled on the Caravan. The following week, I saw another Odyssey at a different dealership at a lower price. The Caravan was fine, but I hated that car the entire time I owned it because I was comparing it to what could have been.

The second goal is purchase price. You must know the fair price of the vehicle before you begin your negotiation. The dealer may show you all kinds of documentation about how much they paid for the car and how much they spent getting it ready for sale, but that is just paper. If the dealer paid too much for the car or it needed extensive repairs, that is not your problem. Use the tools at your disposal to know the market value of the vehicle and hold the dealer accountable for meeting that price. If they insist on making their money back on their mistake, let the buyer who has not read this book be their sucker.

A third goal should be respect. You are making a huge commitment of time and money to this purchase. The person or dealership selling the vehicle is going to make a profit. Do you want to reward someone who is disrespectful? If you feel uncomfortable for any reason, find someone else to do business with.

Think about any other goals you have for the purchase and be steadfast in meeting them. When you meet your goals, you will feel great about the deal.

Cognitive dissonance

The psychological stress or mental discomfort that results when we have two conflicting thoughts or beliefs generally gets resolved by changing one of those thoughts. You cannot believe a used car is worth $15,000 and also believe you got a fair deal if you paid $16,000. Since feeling you got a fair deal is more pleasant that feeling you got screwed, most people simply tell themselves that the car was really worth $16,000 regardless of the empirical evidence to the contrary. This is a fine coping mechanism after the fact, but be wary of this mind trick. The job of every car salesperson is to recalibrate your mind in order to have you believing you are getting a good deal and your mind wants to play along. Cognitive dissonance is the primary reason you should write down your goals for the deal. In the heat of the moment, you may be your own worst enemy.

Tip 3 - Do due diligence

Selecting a dealer

Unless you are a mechanic, you have to trust the person or dealer selling you a car. Dealers have a reputation to maintain, so they have an incentive to be trustworthy. However, they have a stronger incentive to make money and that often results in taking advantage of the uninformed (clearly not you). Years ago, word of mouth was the only check on bad behavior. That has changed dramatically in the Internet age to the benefit of car buyers. When you consider ratings sites, social media sites, and personal blogs there are literally millions of potential data points to consider. Happily, Google has already aggregated most of that information for you. When you search a dealer's name on Google, you will typically see a star rating for the dealer. If the dealership rating is less than three stars, avoid that dealership altogether. They are clearly not a place you want to reward with your business.

If the dealership you are researching is rated three stars or higher, click through to those reviews and read them. If there are too many to read, resort by lowest score first. As you read through the reviews, look for patterns. Often, the bad reviews are from people who did not do their homework complaining about price, but you may find a common theme. If all the bad reviews are about financing and you are getting financed by your credit union, then keep this dealership in your consideration set. If they are lowballing people on their trades and you are selling your car yourself, this may still be a dealership you want to shop. Sometimes all the bad reviews are about a single salesperson, who by this point is probably already fired. On the other hand a lot of good reviews about a particular salesperson gives you a lead on who to ask for.

In addition to the Google reviews, check out Yelp, DealerRater, and the Better Business Bureau. Ideally you will find a dealership with great ratings from all of these sources.

Buying from an individual

New websites and apps designed to help people sell their stuff are popping up every day. Craigslist was the only game in town for awhile, but now Facebook Marketplace, LetGo, OfferUp, and dozens more make person-to-person car sales an easy option for millions of people every year. The person selling their own car may be someone just like you who just wants to get more for the vehicle than a dealer would give them. But consider the market dynamics.

Used car managers at dealerships scour these websites and apps to find cars they can add to their inventory. If a person selling their car is asking too little, these professionals will snap up that vehicle before you ever see it. The cars that remain are either priced too high for a dealer to make any profit or they have something wrong with them that prior shoppers have discovered. If you are buying a used car from a stranger or distant acquaintance, you must take the car to a mechanic for a thorough inspection. If the seller is unwilling to have the car inspected, you can bet there is something wrong with it.

When buying from an individual, even one you think you know well, you should get a Carfax. The Carfax report will show you what types of owner the vehicle had and where it was driven. If the data on the car's history doesn't match the story the seller is telling you, walk away from the deal. If they are lying about when they bought the car and where they got it, then they are probably also lying about how well it has been maintained and why they are selling it.

The risk of buying from an individual demands a discount in the marketplace. The same car sold by a private party will have a lower price than if sold by a dealer simply because many buyers are willing to pay more for the peace of mind at a dealership. If you are willing to do the extra legwork and pay for the Carfax and the mechanical inspection, you can save a little money with a private party deal.

Curbstoners

The draw of a lower price, along with disdain for car dealers brings many people into the private party market. Some shady car dealers take advantage of these people by posing as private individuals. This practice is called curbstoning and it is illegal in many states. However, the loopholes in these laws are big enough to drive a truck through. Why should you care?

The vehicles that these curbstoners sell are usually those cars that the dealer does not want to sell from his lot. These are the cars with problems that would surely cause the dealer pain. Car dealers want to avoid bad reviews or legal battles so they curbstone their junk. If all you know about the seller is a cell phone number, you have no recourse when the car falls apart a month after you buy it.

Spotting a curbstoner is pretty easy. The name of the person selling the car should match the name on the title. If not, walk away. The date on the title should match the seller's story about how long they have owned the car. The Carfax report should show the last owner as a private individual. If the last record on the Carfax report shows a dealer offering the car for sale or the vehicle being sold at an auction, then you can be sure you are dealing with a curbstoner. Do not buy.

Paying for the car

Unless you are buying a car from a close friend or family member, the seller is going to expect full payment. They are not likely to trust your personal check to clear the bank so they will not sign over the title until it does. On the other hand, you are not going to write someone a big check without the title being transferred. There are some escrow services available to facilitate these transfers, but most private party car deals are conducted in cash which puts the buyer at a disadvantage. You are not going to get a refund if the car turns out to be a lemon. Unless that happens within a day or two of the sale, an escrow service will not protect you. So let me reiterate, when buying a used car from an individual you must have the car inspected by a mechanic before you hand over the cash.

Tip 4 - Make an ally

Unexpected kindness

Car salespeople spend their day getting pressured by customers for a better price and getting pressured by their manager to hold gross. The salesperson who "gives a car away" for too little profit will get berated by the boss and teased by their peers. They often get chewed out by customers when they have to deliver the appraisal value on a trade-in, a number they had nothing to do with. All of this conflict can make them mean and cynical, on the inside. Only the ones who can hide their cynicism beneath an endearing smile will last in the business.

However, in order to get a really great deal on a used car, you need the salesperson to be your advocate with the guy or gal in the back room who will decide whether or not to let the car go at your price. If you want them to endure the inevitable chiding from selling a car too cheap, you need to get them on your side.

The best way to do this is to turn the tables on them. Salespeople are trained to establish a rapport with the customer by asking easy questions about your life. Some of the questions are useful to understand what kind of vehicle would best suit your needs, but most of them are just to make you feel more at ease. So why not use the same approach on them? When they ask you a question about your personal life, share the answer, then ask them something about their life. Imagine yourself catching up with a long-lost cousin. Where did they grow up, what high school did they attend, are they a sports fan, what are their hobbies? Making them feel like you care about them will be so out of the ordinary that they will happily stick up for you in the price discussion.

Once they believe you are a really nice person who sincerely cares about them, you can also demonstrate that you know how the business works. Reveal this too early and they might perceive you as confrontational or boasting, in which case they will make it their mission to prove you wrong. But after you have established a good rapport, it will be useful to let them know that you have researched the vehicle history, know how long the vehicle has been in their inventory, and scheduled this appointment on the last day of the month to give them a chance to make their sales goal. If you follow these steps, your salesperson will feel motivated and empowered to stand up to their manager on your behalf.

Tip 5 - Keep your head

Vulnerabilities

Buying a car is exciting. Do not show your excitement. In fact, try and feign mild disappointment. Mr. Spock from Star Trek would not get screwed on a used car deal, that would be illogical. Be Mr. Spock. When you are examining the car, do not say "This is exactly the color I've been looking for." Rather say, "this shade of blue is acceptable." Do not say, "Oh cool, surround sound." Rather say, "hmmm, I don't really listen to music that much." If the salesperson discovers that you really love the car, you will not get the best price.

Buying a car can be confusing. Do not show confusion. You now know the four squares of the deal. You are prepared for anything they throw at you. If you have done your research, lined up your financing, and priced your trade, you know everything you need to know. Be formidable.

Buying a car takes time. Do not get impatient. Customers who walk into a dealership unprepared seldom complete the purchase process in under six hours. Browsing the inventory and taking a couple of test drives can take at least an hour. Having a trade-in appraised takes at least an hour and the person doing the appraisal may not be immediately available. Getting approved for financing can take an hour if you have all the necessary documents with you. Most people do not remember to take their last two pay stubs and last year's tax return to the car dealership. Once you agree to buy the car, it has to be prepared for delivery, which can take an hour if they do a good job of cleaning it up and finding the extra keys. You can expect to spend up to an hour with the F&I manager discussing the extras they rolled into your contract and getting them removed.

This makes for a long day and if you get tired, hungry, and irritated, they expect you to start saying "okay" just to get it all over with. If you find yourself in that frame of mind, leave the dealership.

You probably will not find yourself in this situation because you would never go to the dealership unprepared. First of all, you are splitting up your visit so you took the test drive earlier in the month. You have already arranged financing with your credit union or another lender. Just those two factors will cut several hours off of your final dealership visit. You might also streamline your time by shortcutting the F&I session, but only after you have settled on the final price. The sales manager is not going to be as lenient on the purchase price if he knows ahead of time there is no more money coming to the deal at the F&I desk.

Tricks - key toss, bait & switch

Some car dealers will do just about anything to get you to their dealership and keep you there until you buy a car. The most common trick is advertising a car at a ridiculously low price and unfortunately it is out on a test drive or someone just bought it, but while you're here we have another one just like it only better. A dealership that practices bait and switch tactics does not deserve your business.

Once you get on the lot, the second common trick is the key toss. When you agree to an appraisal on your trade-in and hand your keys over to the dealer, you have effectively given up control of your only means of egress. The dealer has failed in his mission to sell you a car if he is returning those keys and they are always reluctant to give them back. When you are reading reviews of dealerships you will inevitably come across a story of a customer who could not get their keys back until they threatened to call the police. Never agree to an appraisal on your trade until the final visit.

Tip 6 - Find faults

Devalue the car

When a dealership appraises a car, they will point out to you all the little flaws that make the car worth less money. You should do the same when you are evaluating a car to buy. When the salesperson takes you on the walk around before your test drive, point out all of the dings, scratches, wear, and anything else you see, or smell. Feel along the edge of the door for paint seams. A repainted car was a damaged car. Open the hood and check the bolts that attach the fenders. If the bolts are not still under the factory paint, the panels have been removed for some reason. Look for negative factors in the Carfax report. Revealing the problems with the car creates the ammunition your salesperson will need when arguing with the sales manager about your low-ball price offer. You want the salesperson telling the sales manager your offer is generous considering the condition of the vehicle.

Devalue the dealership

You will pay a premium for buying a used car from a dealership versus an individual. Most car dealers believe they deserve that premium because they have more overhead, but their overhead does not create any value for you unless they use it to your benefit. If the dealership has a service department with ASE certified mechanics, did they use that service department to recondition the vehicle? Is that service department close enough and open at times that would be convenient to you in the future? If you say no to those questions, then the dealership's overhead in their service department does not justify a premium on this car.

The other major expense the dealership must cover in their price is advertising. Advertising creates no value for you, other than helping you discover the car. The dealer's advertising should increase demand for the vehicles in their inventory, resulting in faster sales at higher prices. But the vehicle you are considering is still sitting on the lot on the last day of the month. The advertising the dealer paid for did not work for this car or it would already be gone. You should not be paying a premium to subsidize the dealer's ineffectual marketing.

The only other factor that does justify the dealer's premium over a private party sale is peace of mind. If the car breaks down just days after you buy it, the dealer should be willing to stand behind his product and fix the problem. That is not always the case. Car dealers mark their used cars "AS IS" to protect themselves from this obligation. A dealer may repair a recently sold vehicle at no charge, but that is not because they are legally obliged to do so. A dealership should be willing to provide a written guarantee for at least the first month of ownership. If they are not willing to provide this peace of mind, they do not deserve a premium over the private party price.

Tip 7 - Read every line

The Devil is in the details

The last step in your used car purchase will be the most challenging. Nearing the end of an arduous process, having negotiated a great price for the car, you will be eager to claim the spoils of victory and celebrate. This is when you are most vulnerable. Nothing you agreed to before signing the final contract is binding. The only truth is what ends up in your paperwork.

Most of the documents in the giant stack of papers are boilerplate documents mandated by state laws. You should pay attention to these documents, but the dealer cannot alter these without risking jail time. The problem is that there are so many of them that you just get into a groove. The two documents you must look for are the actual bill of sale and the finance contract. This is where the actual purchase price you negotiated should appear.

The person having you sign all of these documents is also encouraging you to buy extras and may have thought so highly of their own salesmanship that they went ahead and factored in those costs. Do not sign a bill of sale or finance contract that has a different price than the one you negotiated. On the finance contract, make sure the interest rate and any fees are what you expect. If you have pre arranged financing with a credit union or bank, make sure the dealership has not included their normal finder's fee. They did not arrange your financing so should not be getting the fee they normally charge.

Finally, make absolutely sure that the amount you are financing is equal to the price you negotiated minus the down payment and any equity from your trade-in. This math is straightforward, but somehow gets altered on far too many deals. Bring your calculator and your resolve. Now that you know what to look for, you should emerge unscathed.

Bonus Tip

Ask a friend

Thank you for spending this time preparing for your used car purchase. I hope you enjoyed learning about the used car deal. The average used car buyer undertakes this process only a few times in their life, while car dealers do it all day every day. Going up against a pro without this knowledge would be like a little leaguer trying to hit a Max Scherzer slider. There is a lot to remember and if you are unsure about any of it, I offer this final tip. Ask a friend. I'm eager to answer any further questions and look forward to hearing your story. Just hop on the website or find me on LinkedIn to share.

www.ingramcontent.com/pod-product-compliance
Lightning Source LLC
Chambersburg PA
CBHW030044230526
45472CB00005B/1665